VINTAGE

VARAVARA RAO

Varavara Rao has been a poet, literary critic, public speaker and teacher of language and literature. He is the author of seventeen collections of poetry and nineteen books of prose (including seven books of literary criticism and translation), all in Telugu. The collection of his prison letters, *Captive Imagination* (2010), was published by Penguin.

N. Venugopal is a poet, literary critic, journalist, public speaker and translator with thirty-two books, both in Telugu and English and as many in translation, to his credit. Leaving his mainstream journalism career, including the *Economic Times* and the *New Indian Express*, after over twenty years, he has been editing his own alternative small venture, *Veekshanam*, a monthly journal of political economy and society, for the last twenty years.

Meena Kandasamy is an activist, poet, novelist and translator. Her books of poetry include *Touch* and *Ms Militancy*, and she is the author of three acclaimed novels, *The Gypsy Goddess*, *When I Hit You* and *Exquisite Cadavers*. In 2022, she was elected as a fellow of the Royal Society of Literature (FRSL) and was also awarded the PEN-Germany's Hermann Kesten Prize for her writing and work as a 'fearless fighter for democracy, human rights and the free word'.

Her latest published work is *The Book of Desire*, a translation of the love poetry of Thirukkural, and her own political poetry pamphlet, *Tomorrow Someone Will Arrest You*.

Celebrating 35 Years of
Penguin Random House India

VARAVARA RAO

RAO

A Life in Poetry

Edited by **N. Venugopal** & **Meena Kandasamy**

VINTAGE

An imprint of Penguin Random House

VINTAGE

USA | Canada | UK | Ireland | Australia
New Zealand | India | South Africa | China

Vintage is part of the Penguin Random House group of companies
whose addresses can be found at global.penguinrandomhouse.com

Published by Penguin Random House India Pvt. Ltd
4th Floor, Capital Tower 1, MG Road,
Gurugram 122 002, Haryana, India

Penguin
Random House
India

First published in Vintage by Penguin Random House India 2023

ISBN 9780143463160

Typeset in Monticello LT Pro by Manipal Technologies Limited, Manipal

www.penguin.co.in

Contents

INTRODUCTION
MEENA KANDASAMY

MY FIRST ENCOUNTER WITH VARAVARA RAO

My first memory of encountering the name 'Varavara Rao' was in the newspapers. This was in the early 2000s, when warring guerrilla groups came to peace-talks tables. As a young Tamil woman, I consistently followed the Norway-brokered talks between the Liberation Tigers of Tamil Eelam (LTTE) and the Government of Sri Lanka. Likewise, I was fascinated by what was happening on home ground: the talks between People's War and the Indian government. Perhaps because of the way in which the print media at that time both valorized and demonized the guerrilla fighters, I was fascinated that three people had dared to be emissaries between the governments and the fighters. One of the interlocutors was Varavara Rao, the other two were Gaddar and Kalyan Rao. Growing up in a household without television, I would wake up every morning and read about the progress in these talks as if it were a serialized novel. (Both talks ended in failure; in both cases the state used the ruse of the talks to go on a spate of naked aggression.) To my younger self, being an interlocutor seemed like an act of absolute courage and immense responsibility. At that time, little would I have imagined that one day in my life, I would get the opportunity to work with the poetry of this fierce, larger-than-life poet.

My second memory of encountering Varavara Rao's name was during a particularly traumatic episode in my brief marriage. The man I married was a self-professed Maoist; he asked me to read aloud a particular poem of Varavara Rao: 'Photo'. The poem speaks about the risks that await were a revolutionary's photo to fall into the hands of the police. 'I lost all my desire for a photo,' he writes and equates the smell of a burning photograph to the 'stench of/ iron heels and brutal feet/The stink of khaki dress'. Knowing that my (then) husband was looking for validation for his poetic tastes, I said something to the effect that 'this poem strikes deep'. I savoured the poem, little aware that it was going to be a precursor to something very sinister. I did not realize that this poem would form the philosophical basis for my abuser embarking on a process of my erasure. Upholding this poem by Varavara Rao as the truest example of a poet committed to the revolution, he would taunt me.

'Why this narcissism? Why do your photos float around on Facebook? Do you realize that if we were to ever go underground, we would be haunted by all these pictures of you that are everywhere?'

Such intellectual bullying would be followed by strict, supervised action: I would be forced to delete my pictures from social media, from my own laptop, from my website, from wherever they existed. Because: a future threat, the fear of the state, the fear of repercussion. Those terrors lay in the faraway unknown, but the terror of displeasing a violent man was immediate. I did as told, believing that my obedience would pave way to his kindness. It did not. These days, as I poke around my Internet presence, trying to find my pictures before 2011, I remember this poem. Written by a radical poet to call out state surveillance and intimate memory, I had the misfortune of inhabiting a lived reality where these powerful lines were deployed to serve the purpose of a toxic-masculine act of female erasure. For the many years that followed, I associated the name Varavara Rao with a painful memory; the poet had no role to play in the emotive violence inflicted on me, and yet, his words were appropriated to serve the most unintended cause.

Subsequently, I would come across Varavara Rao's name in the usual, predictable ways: an invitation to a conference of leftist writers, or the signatory to a petition condemning the state one way or another. In 2018, when I was away teaching in New York and pregnant with my second child, I read news of my friend Rona Wilson's arrest. This time Varavara Rao's name also surfaced—as someone who was under the state's scanner in the same infamous Bhima Koregaon conspiracy case. He was also arrested. It was during his time in jail that I established touch with N. Venugopal and the idea of this anthology became concrete. Reading Venugopal's book, *Varavara Rao: An Intimate Portrait by a Nephew*, I learnt that Varavara Rao has spent close to a decade in various prisons around the country, beginning with his first arrest in 1973. He has been implicated in more than twenty-five cases, often under various draconian anti-terror legislations such as the Maintenance of Internal Security Act (MISA), the National Security Act (NSA), the Terrorist And Disruptive Activities (Prevention) Act (TADA) and the Unlawful Activities Prevention Act (UAPA), but the prosecution has never been able to prove a single charge in a single case against him.

Varavara Rao is perhaps the most-jailed poet in independent India's history. He also holds the distinction for being the only poet to have voluntarily opted to cancel his own bail (in the Secunderabad Conspiracy Case) and instead choose imprisonment. So severe were the threats to his life from state forces that he 'forfeited the borrowed freedom on bail in order to enjoy the freedom of writing and the security of life'. At the time of this incident, Varavara Rao embodied the angry young man; he was in his early forties. Today, he is double that age (in his eighties), but his fiery verses sparkle with the same rage. Penguin had already published his previous collection of letters written from jail, so they seemed like a natural choice for us. I thank our editor Elizabeth Kuruvilla for her endearing patience, clarity and support in working through this book, and ensuring that it sees the light of day, however difficult the circumstances.

Before I leave you with the incredible political poetry of Varavara Rao, I wish to share some of my thoughts on his work by way of an introduction.

A NOTE ON TRANSLATING VARAVARA RAO

I begin with a note on translation because this edited volume contains the work of nine different translators, including Venugopal and me—each of them with a distinct style, each of them having a bearing on how Varavara Rao is received in English. Here I wish to acknowledge all of the translators for their work: Venugopal, Rohith, J.C., K.V.R, K. Balagopal, V. Mohana Prasad, D. Venkat Rao and K. Damodar Rao.

The illustrious history of Telugu poetry spans over a millennium, however, the genre of free-verse dates back to only a century. Varavara Rao's poetry is a hybrid of tradition and modernity. 'Pre-modern Telugu poetry, with a peculiar prosody named padyam of four lines in metre, depended mostly on sound at the cost of meaning and feeling also. The modern free-verse movement beginning 1930s fought against the tradition and brought meaning and feeling to the fore with free flow of expression. However, the modern poetry continued to retain sound elements like rhythm, rhyme and alliteration,' explains Venugopal. It was in this context that Varavara Rao, whose work has roots in classical Telugu poetry, evolved as a champion of modern literature and free-verse in the 1960s. How does this hybridity pose a challenge? Translating only free-verse from one language to another is relatively easy but attempts to reproduce the sound—a remnant from Varavara Rao's classical training—is an arduous, impossible task.

Tracing the evolution of Varavara Rao's poetry, we need to pay attention to the fact that after a decade of poetry, he became a lecturer and a public speaker. Venugopal, co-editor of this volume, says that since the 1970s, both public speaking and poetry became Varavara Rao's means of communication. There is an interchangeability in how he deploys these distinct forms. Venugopal adds, 'Thus his poetry, many a time, can be read as a conversation, a debate, a speech, an exposition. At times it may appear as a series of different metaphors describing the same subject, like in a speech. Bringing this style and tone into translation is difficult.'

When Venugopal and I worked on this volume, we also realized that all of Varavara Rao's poems were invariably a product of history, a reaction to one political incident or another, a chronicle of an outrage, an ongoing diary. As editors of his volume, we faced a conundrum: shorn of context, these poems would convey little to a reader; saddled with context, the poems would lose their essential lightness of touch. We have tried to work around this by providing annotations wherever required. These will allow a reader to access the historical backdrop against which the poems were written. We decided against working such information into the body of the poem as we firmly believe that such editorial interference would simply kill the poem. Here, I have to thank Venugopal for his single-handed devotion to the poet-subject; without his dedicated efforts we would not have this book in the present form.

Even as we meditate on the effectiveness of the translations into English, we have to pay attention to how Varavara Rao's poetry operates in the Anglophone domain in India. The somewhat sanitized, almost elitist leanings of Indian Writing in English stand in stark contrast to the verses of Varavara Rao. He once said in an interview, 'Even the mainstream Telugu dailies publish revolutionary writings.' Through this edited volume, we have taken the first steps in staking claim and space for such radical writings to also become part of the Anglophone imagination and cultural sphere in India.

VARAVARA RAO'S POLITICS

As founding-member of the Viplava Rachayitala Sangham (Revolutionary Writers Association, known by its shorter, popular name Virasam), Varavara Rao's history is deeply intertwined with far-left politics. An editorial in *Economic and Political Weekly* (1986) notes, 'It was Varavara Rao's multi-faceted role as an intellectual committed to the Marxist-Leninist movement in Andhra and his unrelenting creative spirit, despite years of hardship, that has made him a target of state agencies.' As India's most-incarcerated poet, it is little wonder that a significant portion of his poems which appear in this volume were either written in, and/or deal with prisons.

Varavara Rao's clarity of thought and feisty debunking of neoliberal propaganda occupy the same place in his poetry as they do in his public speeches. In a world where even the most radical thinkers hide behind obfuscation, his strength lies in his simplicity. I remember watching an interview he had given before his arrest, where he brings up the point: 'People question our categorization of India as a semi-feudal society. Untouchability exists today, what greater evidence do we need for calling our society semi-feudal?'

How does Varavara Rao navigate his privilege (he was born a Brahmin), his positionality (anti-caste rhetoric) and the limit of identity politics (he is an avowed communist)? Although this book is not about the political moorings of Varavara Rao, I cannot help but single out one instance to observe that he was supportive of the reservation policy decades before it became acceptable and cool enough for the Indian communists to take such a stance. Running into several pages, his poem 'Déjà Vu' (1986) condemns in no uncertain terms an agitation led by upper class, upper caste youth of Andhra Pradesh against a state-level commission's recommendation for increase in reservation. A quarter century before we saw Delhi media lap up the *Youth For Equality* protests and give non-stop coverage to the horrific demand that reservations should not be given to the backward classes, Varavara Rao captured the rot in the heart of India's journalistic cabals:

Everybody was delighted
[. . .] Newspapers?
Oh, absolutely thrilled!
[. . .]
Media persons are 'merit' creatures
Their camera hearts 'click'
Their pens shriek
'Youthful brilliance!'

His criticism of Manuvad, or Brahminical Hindutva, alongside his takedown of capitalism and the oppressive state machinery makes him essential reading for everyone trying to grapple with the question of social justice and democracy in India today. Varavara Rao calls out the system for its intrinsic unfairness (how can the Brahmin be born of the head and the Shudra of the feet, he said in an interview once), and for its mindless advocacy of violence (such as in his poems).

His poems also alert us to the violence unleashed on the religious minorities in this country. In 'Homecoming' (2017), he writes:

They remove and throw away
The skull caps from the heads
As they would sever heads from torsos
They pull beards, blame mullahs.

To say they acted like beasts,
Charging at others for the crime of eating beef
Is indeed an insult to beasts.

Distrust of the state, anger against the police machinery, lamentation of the prison system—these are recurring themes in Varavara Rao's poetry. As I worked on this volume, I felt that his revulsion towards the role of the state came from two intertwined facets. The first was the killings, police firings, attacks and imprisonments which he had witnessed first-hand. The second reason was explicitly his ideological moorings.

More than a hundred years ago, while in hiding in August 1917, Lenin wrote in *State and Revolution*:

> The state is an instrument for the exploitation of the oppressed class by the ruling class, a machine for the oppression of one class by another, a tool in the hands of the ruling class for suppressing the resistance of the oppressed class. The bourgeoisie needs the state in order to maintain its domination over the working class, and the capitalist state, in its turn, is an instrument for the domination of the bourgeoisie over the working people.
>
> Thus, the state is not a neutral force standing above society; it is a force for the maintenance of class rule. In bourgeois society, the state serves to protect the interests of the capitalist class, and this fact is disguised by the 'democratic' forms of the state. The capitalist state claims to represent the 'general interests' of society, but in reality, it represents only the interests of the ruling class.

Routinely calling out the state as a tool of the ruling class and a stooge of the bourgeoise, his poetry offers the metaphorical frame which helps us understand how the state's policies, actions and machinery perpetuate inequality and injustice. The endless list of the state's repressive strategy—censorship, surveillance, violence, terror—are routinely catalogued in Varavara Rao's work, poetry serving the space of chronicle and reading almost as if they were charged, urgent political pamphlets. His poems span several decades and were written under wildly different political regimes— yet, reading through the annotations, we get the feeling that the more things change, the more they remain the same. In other words, history repeats itself. This sheds light on why Varavara Rao is disillusioned with electoral parties in general; his poetry focuses instead of how any political party in power operates as a repressive state, and the iron fist with which the state machinery has handled people's uprisings and social justice movements.

In his poem, 'Poetry' (1987), he writes,

'You go on about surveillance
Poetry gets ignited and continues to fire.
You go on about governance
Poetry talks about people even in sleep.
[. . .]
Poetry is an open secret — the state ceases to exist
As poetry takes shape in my heart.'

In these evocative lines Varavara Rao sings of the enduring power and relevance of poetry in the face of surveillance and propaganda. The unwavering resilience of poetry breaks through the neoliberal speak of 'good governance', transcends boundaries, manages to voice people's concern even when it is pushed into a dormant sleep-state.

This theme of what poetry can achieve, and how it ought to be written runs through Varavara Rao's work. These lines from his poem 'What We Need Is Poetry' (2013), which appears later in this volume, imbibe the style of a hoarse party-pamphlet. Here, there is an enumeration of what kind of poetry we need:

The poetry with a spine
That can stand up to the system
And hold it accountable,
The poetry that refuses power
The poetry that challenges the state.

Poetry, in his envisioning, manages to simultaneously challenge, bypass and dismantle the state. Constructed as an open secret—as the truth that needs no telling—it renders the state irrelevant as it refuses power even as it claims the space for its self-creation within the poet's heart (a territory that cannot be ceded to the state).

Here it also becomes imperative to realize that the oppressive ruling classes and the state have not only seized resources and power, they have also seized narrative. Things spoken by the state or the capitalist class has moved from the banality of absolute falsehood uttered during the days of the Emergency, into the posh public relations communication campaigns of today. In what is an international phenomenon, lobbyists specializing in crisis communication enable genocide-washing. How do we the people reclaim this narrative?

In his poem, 'Assassination of Satyam' (1970), Varavara Rao writes,

See if it is really the truth that is dead,
It is the government that is saying that
the truth has died. The government that
lied at every step of its making,
in the Parliament, at the court, saving its face
from the entanglements of law.

It is those who turned days and nights
Upside-down, those whose job is to legitimize
Exploitation in the name of representing people,
Those who dismantled the houses of the labourers,
Those who drank blood for their own pleasure,
Can they even see the truth?
Can they ever know the greatness of truth?

Society, in the eyes of this radical poet, is not just caught at the crossroads of the struggle for justice, but it also has battle lines drawn in the struggle to reclaim the truth. We can find this theme appearing in several other poems, including 'Livewire Is Better Than a Poet' (1968), 'The Poet Is No Lion But a Stream' (1976), 'The Truth' (1977) and 'Chains Write Now' (1977). Perhaps because Varavara Rao imagines the role of the poet as a truth-teller, there is a brutal directness in his verses. What he intends to communicate does not have to be hidden under the shadow of metaphors. For truth to be explosive, it does not require subtlety or sophistication—and we witness this in all of his verses.

WHERE HAS THE PUPPY GONE?

The puppy has died
The nice young dog has gone away.
Why do my hands seek something?

What is this? In the past, a biscuit held this way
Would have gone in a flash.
Today it angrily stares at me
The pup that played with me.
Where has it gone?
Leaving me alone?

I can believe people die.
They have heaven
Beautiful angels, divine flowers
Ambrosia—everything is there for them.
I know that's why people pray
In this world, to attain another world.
That's why they go, leaving
The warmth of the mother's lap
The tight embrace of a son and
The sweetness of the beloved's kiss.
But tell me, why should a puppy leave?

Where can it go?
How can such a truthful life

---

* 'kukkapilla ekkaDikani veLipOtundi?' from *Chalinegallu,* Swechchasahiti,
 Warangal, 1968
 This is one of Varavara Rao's earliest poems, written on the death of a pet
 dog at the house of a classmate's uncle.

Vanish into thin air?
No, it's a lie . . .
Maybe some selfish thief came in my absence
And it might have gone chasing him.
It would chase those greedy people until
    the other world and
Descend on the portico like a cloud by dawn.
Yes, what's there for the puppy
In that heaven that it would stay there?

In the puppy's eyes
I will read the class struggles in heaven.

1958
Translated by N. Venugopal

DON'T FEAR, DAWN BREAKS OUT

Why is this night heavy with drowsiness?
Why is this earth murmuring in its sleep?
White flowers of the parijata fall down
As liberated tears of a lotus-eyed lady.
Using their plaited hair, all the river virgins
Tie the neck of the roaring sea.
Lady Night is dozing with her head on
The ocean's expansive lap.
Hiding themselves from the devils
The sleeping scientists in the burial ground
Conspire for some hopeful words.

As if the problems of life
And its struggles are not enough
The bones of the intellectuals in the graveyard
Rub against each other.
Hatred for the dead, unconcerned and uncourteous
Fumes like sulphur.
The wild plant on the grave of a Hindu lover
Tries in vain to feel the perfume of
The rose on the beautiful tomb of a Muslim beloved.

---

* 'bhaLluna tellavaaruninka bhayam lEdu' from *Chalinegallu*,
Swechchasahiti, Warangal, 1968
Another early poem, read at a poet's meet when he was eighteen. It
received wide acclaim, made him known as a poet with promise. The
first part, in archaic expression, talks about the gloomy atmosphere all
around, and the second part, in modern language, speaks of optimism.
The poem symbolizes the mood of the youth in the first decade after
decolonization.

Tears of the worried son
Who could not wipe his mother's tears
Are tired, unable to extinguish the pyre.
The vulture raises its wing as
The waiting fox growls in the night of the owls.

With that kick
Ashes fall in the eye of silence.
Cicadas squeak in the ears like hammer blows.
A historic chamber of devils is held on the tree.
A bear has torn the breast of a passer-by on the hill.
The cobra from its hole hisses and raises its hood.
The beggar in the street is allowing
The earthly cold to eat his bones
Though he doesn't have a gulp of gruel.

Why, having not expected
The night to be so horrible
Why, having not expected
The world to be so abominable
I dreamed of my favourite desire.
Hoping that the night means
A darkness full of the moon
Lotuses fanned by a pleasant breeze
White and lovely moonshine everywhere.
For the lovers to be content
Jasmines and flowers
Koels and damsels
Swung in the dreamy world.
Hoping that the world means whiteness
Men with kind hearts

Ideals reaching the heights of skies
The upright people who detest injustice . . .

That's all humbug.
I never expected the night to be so terrible.
Now there is only one desire:
To wait like this night
In the hope of a rising dawn.

There is a stir beyond the mountainous barriers of caste.
See, the shades of blood harvest
Fragmented rays behind the hill.
Now, there is no place for fear.
Certainly, the dawn will come.

If it dawns
I will separate black and white exactly.
I will assess good and bad impartially.

Has anybody, really any one of you
Seen into the face of the burning sun?
How can you portray him without ever seeing him?
Tomorrow
I will challenge his arrows of light.
And look straight into his red eyes.
Tomorrow I have to gauge
The ratio of redness and warmth in him.

No need to fear, dawn will break.
Not only into the simple sun's face
Not only into the sun's face alone.

Tomorrow, I will look into every face on earth.
I will speak out their wrongs and my grudges to their faces.
I will look into everybody's eyes with clear eyes.
I will make them vomit dirt hidden behind their eyes.
I will transmit X-rays into their souls.

Dawn will break, don't fear.
Tomorrow is an auspicious day—the sun will shine red.
Tomorrow the pyre of sins will burn red.
Tomorrow peace will cover the whole world.

1958
Translated by N. Venugopal

MARILYN MONROE

Every part of your body defines beauty.
Every gesture of yours proclaims youth.

Gorgeous woman
Looking at your heavenly beauty
The world is spellbound.
You too left your mouth half-opened
Perhaps to explain the secrets
Of that celestial magnificence.

Your lips that lit fires
In so many hearts
That it never met
Burnt on the pyre.
Perhaps to show your heart

Age has sculpted curves and attractions
In every part of your body.
But could not take away
The innocence contained
In your childlike eyes and gentle heart.

---

* 'akavitaavastuvu?' from *Chalinegallu*, Swechchasahiti, Warangal, 1968
  This poem is a response to a sneering comment made by a literary
  associate after Marilyn Monroe's suicide, on whether she could be a
  worthy theme for poetry. The poem itself doesn't directly refer to her, but
  when first published in the monthly journal *Jyothi*, it was accompanied
  by a note on and a line drawing of the actress. Both were removed when
  the poem was included in the poet's first collection.

Your serene heart suffered betrayal
Expecting a charming experience
From this decadent society, which is
Drowned in greed and belligerence.

You know,
This world grabs light produced by Niagara
But never considers how that fire was born.
Falling from such a high altar
Breaking the magnanimous heart of water.

Human psyche developed
From puppet play to running machines
But has not moved an inch
In understanding compassion.
Maybe that's why you could not settle anywhere.

You radiated for a while
Just like lightning on the faces of bloated clouds.
Your presence for that moment
Is still raining gold.

But still
You have not yet become
A 'sacred' subject to write about.
We grind our mouths till they tire
To gossip of rumours and slander against you.

Don't they say that
Stones and pebbles and even shoes of Ram
Got life and gave rise to epics?
But you, a complete human being

A symbol of sex to boot
You are not worthy of poetry!

This society wants to see you nude
But detests your heart from
Appearing unclothed, poignant and unblemished.

This world has closed its eyes
To the splendour of your heart
Which enhanced the elegance of your body.
That's why your sleepless eternal search
     for peace of mind
Resulted in that beautiful long slumber . . .

1962

Translated by N. Venugopal

HUNGER?

O, stupid beggar woman!
Your breath nudges me from behind.
Lacking the touch of youth
It speaks only of your hunger.
Your gaze showered
Across my body lacks all lust
Only your burning hunger.

From your dreams
Of course not the present ones
But when you were a virgin
You saved not even a drop of milk in your breasts.
Not to speak of nectar
To feed your own child.
Now what is left in you to cover
That can't be exploited by groping, greedy men?

But then, what is there to cover?
Really, what can cover you?

None of your drops of blood had a chance
To turn into a drop of milk for your child.

I could not turn myself to see you.
But what should I taste
From your knees poking my calves

---

* 'aakali?' from *Chalinegallu*, Swechchasahiti, Warangal, 1968

Your breasts that could not fully touch
My back, however much you tried
Your eyes that I could not see
And the dirt in your soiled nails
In the hand that you stretched from behind?

Yes, you were hopeful
      seeing my flamboyance.
But I felt sorry that
I did not even have some coins in my pocket
For you to steal without anybody seeing.

Foolish woman
You have sold your youth so cheap.
For your food
I, for my own stomach's sake
Am unable to buy even that cheap youth.

Forgive me
I am not rich enough to embrace you, to feed you.
I do not even have a small coin to offer generously.
In this journey
Where is the guarantee that I will repay
Even if you provide on credit?

1964
Translated by N. Venugopal

LOST CHILD

Where are you, my child?
I am unable to figure out.

I wanted to protect you
No matter what happened
But pleasure tasted sweeter . . .

I know, my experience knows.
What a conflict!
How my blood curdled!
How much pain I suffered
To give shape to you within me.
How do I express my experience in that moment?
How much is the joy bestowed by spring to
The tree agitated by winds in Phalgun!

Every moment that you took shape in me
Your beautiful appearance was as much as
The pain that multiplied in my twisted and troubled veins.
What is this torment
Before the exhilarating moment?
Does the clear sky remember
The dark clouds that covered it
and burst a little earlier?

That's all.

---

* 'tappipOyina SiSuvu' from *Jeevanadi*, Emesco Publishers, Vijayawada, 1971

After that I don't know where I might have thrown you.
In which dirt you may be playing.
The deep desire again kindles
To bear and give birth to you in a new form.
Even before my exquisite creation was done
The kid I saw in my dreams came before my eyes.

How far have you gone?
Where are you?
In which dirt are you playing?
I hope you are playing
Among flowers or flowery souls
Even if you don't get enough food.

Here I am thinking of living, civilized
Among overcrowded beasts and buses.
You may be wallowing on fresh sand dunes
On the banks of a stream
As if you don't care for your body.
My fondness for my body has not diminished even in my solitude.

Honey, how I lost you after bearing so much?
Can you recognize me in this world?
Honour draws a dividing line between you and me.

But then, why should you enter this filth again?
Even I cannot break these chains and extend my heart freely.

Yes, my tender child
Which mother has sacrificed for her own creation
To be forgiven by the entire creation
If the affection for her offspring doesn't flow as milk in her blood?

Why should the child grieve for the mother?

I am the twig that looks at the flower it bore
But cannot express its pleasure.
Only when a honey bird sings sweet in the wind
I fervently desire to fly in search of you. But where are you?

All the dreams of youth
All troubles experienced till now
All tears shed in the past
Only led to giving birth to you.
How proud I would have been.

But today after throwing you off
I am being punished, not for the pleasure
Of giving birth to you, but for that crime.
For the helpless inability to foster you
I am being penalized.
I am able to fill my stomach
By accepting the yoke that divided us.

A branch that raises a new twig
Waves in the wind with joy
The brush that draws a new picture.
Even children become happy mothers in play
Building tiny dollhouses.
What if you are ugly?
You are my offspring
You are my creation.

1965
Translated by N. Venugopal

THE PULSE

What if I sleep in despair
And awake in hope?
I am the leader of my generation
I am the singer, the voice of my epoch.

What if I taste the fruits of my daydreams
Only in my dreams at night?
What if my eyes are soaked in blood
And sweat pours all day long?
I am the one who has not lost faith
In tomorrow's light.

I know I am giving words
To the unrest around me
And rousing the rage within me
For tomorrow's peace
And tomorrow's light.

Countless vague ideas seek
Expression in my letters.

The sun, which has not yet risen
Except in the stirring of my black brother
Burns inside me.

---

* 'jeevanaaDi' from Jeevanaadi, Emesco Publishers, Vijayawada, 1971

That man, my heir
desires not destruction
but radical change . . .
In this or that hemisphere
Africa or Asia
Europe or America
Am I the only hope still left
In this world for the hapless ones
Down and out
In hunger, in unfulfilled desire?

What does it matter if
it is unripe and indistinct?
I am but giving voice to my time
Moved with passion and emotion from the depths of my heart.

I am the electric power
Born in this Operation Generator.
I am aglow.
I am not born like the lamps of old
Trusting in god to burn even in the open.

I can make the molecule dance, the atom sing.
I can realize the progress of the world.

And I shall have my triumph
Inscribed by the rocket on the moon.

What if my life-breath goes out
After lighting a thousand lamps?
I am the radiance of this age.

I am electric power
Born out of Operation Generator.
I am the harbinger of change.

1965

Translated by N. Venugopal

LIVEWIRE IS BETTER THAN A POET

What is it that poets have achieved since time immemorial?
Except revealing some fantastic falsehood
Or covering truth in symbolism
So as not to hurt the unjust?

Whether it was appreciation or disapproval
Admonition or blessing
It was an inability all the way
To taste like salt
To generate heat like fire
To spread air like trees
To pour rain like water.

Radical turned into rhetoric
Fearlessness to foolishness
Poetry as eccentricity
Of no concern to anybody.

But has any poet lived
Like a turbulence attracting the attention of others
Like a deluge of blood in the veins
Like a shock that wakes up the heart
Like a person who is a path-breaker?

The search in poetry is not with a torch
But the poet has to become a shovel.

---

* 'kavikannaa karenTuteega goppa' from *Jeevanaadi*, Emesco Publishers,
  Vijayawada, 1971

To blast the darkness that invisibly spreads in life
The poet has to be a light that calls out voices from the well.

Poetry is not just a message.
There's no escape by pleading that it was just poetry.
Poetry is hope in the eyes of human beings.
It is compassion in the minds of human beings.
There is no self-deception greater than
Separating poetry and life.

If a poet is one who expresses fabulously on paper alone
Livewire would be better than a poet.

1968
Translated by N. Venugopal

ASSASSINATION OF SATYAM

They said they murdered Satyam, the truth!

The truth of the embers sparkling
In the hearts of the slaving poor.
The truth of the heart of the forest.
The truth of the homes of the mountains.

The truth of the sadness of the raging
Class struggle buried in the depths of the valley
That even the sun neglected.
The truth released from the bow of an Adivasi
Directed at the heart of landlords or moneylenders.

Oh, the fool! He thinks he has slayed the truth.

See if it's really the truth that is dead.
It is the government that is saying that
The truth has died. The government that
Lied at every step of its making,

---

* 'satyamvadha' from *Ooregimpu,* Udyama Sahiti, Karimnagar, 1974
Satyam, literally meaning truth, is also a common name of a person in
Telugu. Here, the poet uses it in two senses: as truth and as a reference
to the leader of the Srikakulam tribal peasant struggle, Vempatapu
Satyanarayana, who was popularly known as Satyam. The Srikakulam
tribal uprising began as a demand for tribal rights over land and forest
in the late 1950s, and turned into an armed struggle in 1968 after failed
attempts of appeals to government. Satyanarayana, a teacher hailing
from a tribal community, led the tribals through peaceful and militant
struggles, finally joining the Naxalbari path. He was killed in July 1970.

In the Parliament, at the court, saving its face
From the entanglements of law.

It is those who turned days and nights
Upside down, those whose job is to legitimize
Exploitation in the name of representing people.
Those who dismantled the houses of the labourers
Those who drank blood for their own pleasure
Can they even see the truth?
Can they ever know the greatness of truth?

In the conflict between falsehood and truth
Truth has been killed.

1 October 1970
Translated by Rohith

SAB THEEK HAI

You ask me
If it is hard for me here.
Yes, when I think of those comrades
Who in exile are suffering hardship
To wipe off the misery of the people
My own inertia is hard to bear.

You ask me
If I am happy here.
Hope for the future glimmers
Like lightning within a cloud
In the hearts of the millions of this vast country
It chimes in these fetters.

Even in these wide-mouthed prison dens
Which seek to swallow revolution
There is unrest
Giving the slip

---

* 'sab Theek hai' from *Swechcha*, Yuga Prachuranalu, Hyderabad, 1978
'Sab Theek Hai' (all is well) is a periodical shout-out by night guards at
the checkposts on four sides of the jail. This poem was written during
the poet's second incarceration between May 1974 and April 1975,
when he was arrested in the Secunderabad Conspiracy Case, involving
a number of crimes spread over four years in Telangana. Each of the
crimes is attributed to have happened with the provocation of a poem, a
song, an essay, a short story or a speech, and six writers, including the
poet, were thus charged, along with over forty activists. The poet–friend
referred to in the poem is M.T. Khan, co-accused in the case, who was
also imprisoned at the same time. The Secundarabad Conspiracy Case,
filed in May 1974, ended in the poet's acquittal in February 1989, after
fifteen years of trial.

To the exploiter's flag on guard.
Each morning
Light and the love of the people
Call to have a word with us.

Birds perched on the barbed wire
Over the prison walls
Jasmines that sprout in the sweat
Of the prisoners
Always hold forth a message
In silence.

The breeze blows in the night
As a poet friend described
The moon gets caught in the barbed wire
Over the prison walls.
And we, after singing and talking
Lose ourselves in the dreams of revolution.

But the poor lonely policemen
Exiled from sleep and shelter
Yawns out every hour
'*Sab theek hai!*'

27 June 1974
Translated by J.C.

WOMAN

Woman!
You birth children . . .
The bloodshed
Of motherhood.

Woman!
You nurse children . . .
The life-giving kindness
Of motherhood.

Woman!
You toil away
In the house, in the kitchen
In the field.

Yet you are a slave
You are the silent shadow
Against the wall of male arrogance
Your individuality imprisoned.

Every pleasure is on sale.
You offer delight.
They want dominance.

The husband, benevolent,
Offers flowers of jasmine,

---

* 'stree' from *Swechcha*, Yuga Prachuranalu, Hyderabad, 1978

A beautiful sari—a barter
For his plunder. The lover
Offers a charmer's smile
And sweet words.
You lose, the men win.
One half of life, you don
The part of grief.

Woman!
Your tears will not crush your oppressor
And bathe your rage in flames of fury.
Speak for your rights.
Step in unison with the marching feet.
Leave the system that treats you as an object.
Become a force, become an individual.
Join hands to overthrow patriarchy.
As the flaming red sun rises
There shall be triumph.

September 1975
Translated by Meena Kandasamy

THE POET IS NO LION, BUT A STREAM

The poet is by no means a lion
But a stream.
It is in the nature of a river
Not only to leap from peaks but
Also to flow steadily in plains
Circumventing the hurdles
Stopping at dams.
And if time favours
Breaking them down and moving on
In branches and in canals.

Some people can only see
A flow in the river
And a motion in her gait.
But they can't see
The nature of her mind
And the explosion in her silence.
Those who mistake the sirens for truth
Can never realize
That there is the heat of the sun
In the protoplasm.
That there is the murmuring song of water
In hundreds of thousands of
Megawatts of electricity.

---

* 'kavi simham kaadu, pravaaham' from *Swechcha*, Yuga Prachuranalu, Hyderabad, 1978

That the fish which swims against the current
Moves about only in water.

20 December 1976
Translated by K.V.R.

THE TRUTH

Can a drop of ink from a poet's pen
Express the truth that a worker's sweat can never utter
The truth that his empty stomach can never utter
The truth that his tears can never utter
The truth that his toiling fists can never utter?

14 February 1977
Translated by K.V.R.

---

* 'chemaTachukkalO puTTindE siraachukka' from *Swechcha*, Yuga
  Prachuranalu, Hyderabad, 1978

CHAINS WRITE NOW

So far
Blooming flowers and perfumes
Made me write.
Now
It is your lies that force me to write
The truth.

So far
Breathless agitations and excitement
Drove me.
Now
Your prison and iron heel
Make me breathless
And turn me fierce.

You invaded my expansive world
Cut it into tiny cells
Kept me immobile
And warned me that if I infringe
You know my hand is in the cell.

---

* 'ippuDu sankeLlu raastunnaayi' from *Swechcha*, Yuga Prachuranalu, Hyderabad, 1978
This poem was written twenty months after his third imprisonment during the Emergency (26 June 1975 to 21 March 1977), when tens of thousands of political activists, thinkers and writers were arrested without any charge under the Maintenance of Internal Security Act. The poem follows Bertolt Brecht's poem 'Bad Time for Poetry' (1938) with an indirect reference to Hitler. 'Dictator', in the poem, is a reference to Indira Gandhi, the then prime minister who had imposed Emergency.

And it is you who tied it down
It is you who broke my pen.

But then you are upset as the
Waves of my dreams are spreading.
As I sit cramped in this dark cell
I am neither the first nor the last
In this path that I have travelled.
My songs have their own feet
As they took birth on that path.
What should I do?
You accuse my dreams
I can only laugh at you!

You raised high walls around me.
So my eyes learnt to look at the world
From the skies.
I always had my eyes on earth.
Your walls made me, an introvert
Rise high into the skies of the winged birds.

As much as you moved away from people
To protect your power
I moved towards the belief that
People, people alone, can destroy fascism.

Even your shadow may not tell you the truth.
It may be saying what you want to hear.
But you are alone in the outside world.
Here inside, I am among countless people.
I am with the strength of my beliefs
With the power of people, like a volcano

That will erupt lava and fumes in the future
Even if it appears silent today.

In this long, silent imprisonment
I am sharpening my thoughts.
Dictator, now my chains are writing
Tomorrow I will sing full-throated in freedom.

14 February 1977
Translated by N. Venugopal

INTELLECTUAL

A tree holds leaves up in the sky
To feed the roots deep in the earth.
Flowers in its green crown
Ripen to fruits that drop
To the ground
Turn to seed
Again.

When crime seizes power
Hunts down people
Holds them criminal—
Anyone who remains silent
Becomes a criminal.

14 February 1977
Translated by K.V.R.

---

* 'mEdhaavi' from *Swechcha*, Yuga Prachuranalu, Hyderabad, 1978

YES, HE TOO IS A MAN

He was called a man when he was born
He was called a man when he grew up
But the day he joined the police to earn his bread
His name became lathi, van and rifle.

He is the bogeyman used to put fear into children
By the hapless mother of his own kids.
He is the target at whom his own children
Join other kids to hurl stones and abuse.

When the stomping of his boots die out
When the sharp crease on his clothes wears out
And his feet touch the ground
And his skin touches the air
He again becomes a man.

When the life cells in the body
That gives love to a woman
And affection to children
Come alive
Behold the khaki dress
Hanging lifeless from the roof.

June 1979
Translated by K. Balagopal

---

* 'avunu, ataDoo manishE' from *Bhavishyatthu Chitrapatam*, Samudram
  Mudranalu, Vijayawada,1986
  This poem was written on the agitation of policemen in Punjab,
  demanding better salaries and working conditions, in May 1978.

PHOTO

I have been longing to have a photo
Since I saw billboards put up
By studio grammarians that
Life is momentary
But a photo is permanent.

Do not know what is going to happen
And I love me so much . . .
I just wanted to capture
The adolescent smile under the budding moustache
The hope in youthful eyes.

A mirror only shows the face as it is.
I wanted to see my appearance as it ought to be
In a photograph.

2

Police started valuing my photo
Since I made friends with students
Started moving among the youth

---

* 'foTO' from *Bhavishyatthu Chitrapatam,* Samudram Mudranalu, Vijayawada, 1986
On the tenth anniversary of the filing of the Secunderabad Conspiracy case, poets, writers and activists held a protest demonstration in front of the Andhra Pradesh Legislative Assembly on 4 July 1984. About fifty protesters were arrested and taken to Gosha Mahal Police Station, where police forcibly took photographs of the arrested and manhandled some who questioned it.

And began loving people.

I had never heard that photos of the fearless
Replace those of the criminals.

When pictures that
Kith and kin, friends and lovers
Preserve as a cherished memory
Are wanted by the police
The jolly mood to give a pose
Is ruined.

3

Where smiles shower as moonlight
They offered urine to quench thirst
Seared youth with cigarette butts.

It is not a photo but
Blazing blood that they hung
On the walls of the lock-up.
They developed the sun in the dark room
Attempting to find out the origin of light.

4

They plucked my moustache in the lock-up.
Remove that photo
They poured acid in my eyes.
Remove that photo
They searched for me with

My live photograph in hand
Hide me in the heart.

Put that photo on the burning lamp
In the dark room
The photo that you touch gently
The photo that you look at secretly near the lamp.

In the vicinity of past recollections
The smell of the burning photo
Is in fact the stench of
Iron heels and brutal feet
The stink of khaki dress.

5

I lost all my desire for a photo.

It is true, a photo lasts long.
But I lost hope in being static.
I want to flow
Living, moving, changing
As a symbol of dying change.

Doesn't any remembrance linger?
Look in the lamp.
Doesn't any symbol remain?
Fix your eyes on to your mind.
Every movement creates
A stir.

6

This is a system
Where taste is a weakness.
Friendship, a spy, who attacks.
Love perceives risk.
People's knowledge is treated as
Something that can be ignited.
This is a society where
Values are upside down.
Here: Even the negatives
In the studio are destroyed.

3 August 1984
Translated by N. Venugopal

BHOPAL

Oxygen, a danger
Sight, darkness
Breast milk, a mortal kiss
Colonialism feeds
Crops of feudalism.

Green revolution
Gurgles life force
On the ground where
It drained the village blood.

Cities are hugger-muggered
By the long arms of multinationals.
Exploiters funnel chimney fumes
Right in the heart of cities.

A time bomb explodes, heart quakes
In the centre of every home
Leaving ashes, blue sights devoid of heat or fire.
The 'hand' passes on a ballot paper
To fingers that fumble in the dark.
Human habitations become crematoriums.

---

* 'bhOpaal' from *Bhavishyatthu Chitrapatam*, Samudram Mudranalu,
Vijayawada, 1986
Written after the worst-ever corporate disaster of gas leakage at Union
Carbide India Ltd's pesticide plant in Bhopal on 2–3 December 1984,
killing more than 3000 people.

A corpse encounters the enemy as a nightmare
With the peace of a rich house.

With irate eyes
With breathless hearts, heaving chests
Tens of thousands rise in revolt.
They are neither alive nor dead
Yet, burning top to toe
They spout fire and brimstone
And declare 'death is none but capitalism'.
The genocide
Reveals the conspiracy of exploiters.

Unless you fell the tree of poison
Lives will be lost.
Capitalism on its deathbed
Inhaling war and exhaling poison gas
Lives will be lost.

January 1985
Translated by V. Mohana Prasad

REFLECTION

I did not supply the explosives
Nor ideas, for that matter.
It was you who trod
Upon the anthill with iron heels
And from that trampled earth
Vengeance was born.

It was you who struck the beehive
With your lathi.
Scattered bees exploded
Against your shaken visage
Blotched red with fear.

When the victory drum started beating
In the heart of the masses
You mistook that for an individual
And trained your guns.
The horizon was torn asunder
In this hour of revolt.

January 1985
Translated by K. Balagopal

---

* 'riflekshan' from *Bhavishyatthu Chitrapatam*, Samudram Mudranalu,
Vijayawada, 1986
The poem was written in District Jail, Secunderabad, when the poet
was arrested on the false charge of distributing explosives to the youth.
The latter were actually protesting on 18 January against the killing of a
youth activist in police custody on 18 December 1984.

THE BUTCHER

I am a vendor of flesh.
If you want to call me a butcher
Then you may as you wish.
I kill animals daily.
I cut their meat and sell it.
Blood to me is a familiar sight.

But I saw
The real meaning of being a butcher.
That young boy's blood congealed
In the fear that gathered in my eyes.
His voice went dumb
With the words that would not leave my lips.

Daily I kill animals with these hands.
Never has the blood touched my heart
But that day the blood spilled not on the street
But on my heart.
Will you wash this blood?

Who among you will extend
A humane hand

---

* 'kasaayi' from *Bhavishyatthu Chitrapatam*, Samudram Mudranalu,
Vijayawada, 1986
Written after hearing the testimony of a butcher, who was witness to
police brutality and the killing of a student activist when the latter was
participating in a strike on 15 May 1985 in Kamareddy, a town in
Nizamabad district.

And unburden my heart
Of the weight of that horrendous sight?

Six lathis broke on his bones
In a mad rage.
The butt of the rifle thrashed his body
To pulp.

Its mouth struck the policeman's jaw.
They said then
That the prostrate youth had attacked with a knife
And there was an 'encounter'.

I too kill animals
But I have never hated them.
I do sell flesh
But never and to none have
I sold myself.

Blood oozes from
The thousand apertures in his body.
The thousand watching eyes are tearful
But his own eyes are dry.
Unlike the goat under my knife
He does not shout 'Ba ba'
He appears to be looking into tomorrow.

Yesterday's sight
No, it is already the day before yesterday's
The scene of the bandh of May 15.
You cannot drive that memory from me
As long as there is breath in my body.

Today I may tell it to you
Because I cannot hide it within me.
Tomorrow I may hide it within me.

Let them destroy my livelihood
But that child
Will haunt me forever.

O, brothers and sisters
We do not kill even a snake like that.
I, who kill goats daily, understood that day
The cruelty that combines and conspires
To take a life.

I am a vendor of flesh
Yes, I am a butcher
The meat of sheep and the meat of goats
I sell for a living.

That minister himself
Gives to policemen
Prizes and promotions
Medals and weighty purses
For taking of human lives.
That the minister means the government.
That the police are our guardians.
Whose government is it and
Whose guardians are they?
The life of that boy
Fleeing into eternity
Told me.
I realized then that

The real butcher is
The state.

9 June 1985

Translated by K. Balagopal

THE BARD

When order is amiss
And billowing pitchy-clouds of time
Strangle the throat
Neither blood trickles
Nor tears drop.

Lightening swirls into thunder
Drizzle surges into a deluge, and
Absorbing the mother's tears of agony
Purl out from prison grille
Voices of the poet's missive.

When the tongue pulsates
Tone manumits the air, and
Song turns missile in battle.
The foe fears the poet,
Incarcerates him, and
Tightens the noose around his neck.
But already, the poet in his notes
Breathes among the masses.

The scaffold
Like a gravitating balance
Disseminates into earth

---

* 'kavi' from *Bhavishyatthu Chitrapatam*, Samudram Mudranalu, Vijayawada, 1986
  Written about the hanging of South African poet and political activist Benjamin Moloise by the apartheid regime on 18 October 1985 at Pretoria Central Prison.

Challenges to death
And hoists the paltry
Hangman colonist.

October 1985

Translated by D. Venkat Rao

AFRAID OF THE EARTH

Heaping threat upon threat
Spreading fear upon fear
He himself got scared.

Got scared of habitations
Of water and even schools.
At last, he was afraid of his own shadow.

He shuddered when wastelands turned into green fields
When a seed blossomed into a plant in the furrow
When plants waved with the wind.

Youngsters made him afraid.
Their imaginations
Their dreams
And their pens, everything made him fearful.

He went on imprisoning freedom
And finally shocked at the sound of chains.

Trembled at the sight of forest

---

* 'bhoomiki bhayapaDi' from *Bhavishyatthu Chitrapatam*, Samudram
Mudranalu, Vijayawada, 1986
Written after hearing and reading about the police destroying memorial
columns in various Telangana districts, particularly in Paidipalli and
Indravelli. In Telangana, it had been a custom since the 1940s to build
columns in memory of those who laid down their lives in people's
struggles, whether killed by police or landlords, or those who died
naturally.

And the Adivasi in the woods
He spilled blood from the singing bamboo
And threatened the flowing Godavari.
With fear, he fired at the vision
Shot dead words and silences.
He bumped off the soul.

Afraid, he killed those who did not fear death.
Afraid of the martyrs
He even destroyed memorial columns with dynamite.

If you blow off the lamps and
Erase the sweet memories of the lamps
Will the sign of struggle go off?

What will happen to this earth
Which gave life to that sign?

This earth
Becoming dark as the lights are put off
Dejected at the demise of the sun
Getting heated up with the burning villages
Provoked by the destruction of memorial columns
What will happen to this earth?

The place where only yesterday
People moved about
Martyrs fell and
Memorial columns rose
With fear, he levelled the ground
Turned it into a graveyard and posted armed guards.

But still, the earth is there, isn't it?
What will that earth say?

13 December 1985
Translated by N. Venugopal

THE DAY OF NAMING

1

Can the empire agree
If uprising makes
The vagrant and untitled
Valiant?
Heroes must have lineage.

When people of the forest converge
Gather mortar, wood and stone
And build, can it become a saga?
History must have a foundation.

Do you light a lamp on the mountain
For the rag-worn
Bullet-torn Gonds?
Lamps must be lit only for the nobility.

2

Indeed, even if I am asked about their hamlet
What can I say?

---

* 'pEru peTTina rOju' from *Bhavishyatthu Chitrapatam*, Samudram
  Mudranalu, Vijayawada, 1986
  Written in jail after reading a news item on the destruction of the
  Indravelli memorial column by the police in 1986. The column was later
  rebuilt by the government. (https://www.thehindu.com/news/national/
  telangana/why-are-adivasis-and-lambadas-fighting-over-indervelli-
  martyrs-column/article61864595.ece)

If I am asked to count
To sixty or thirteen
I can only sight the stars
Whereas you flaunt indemnity lists.

Who would christen the one
Delivered and discarded in the forest?
Maybe
You might have got them first
In (to) the census roll
Or voter's scroll;
Perhaps eliminated from Adilabad hospital,
Or mopped out with the monument today
They cannot aspire for titles.

There
The wood and pit, valley and pinnacle
Bird and reptile, water and fire
Man and beast, field and nest
Darkness and light
All of them bear just (one) name:
The forest.
The forest is both mother and baby to itself.

Alarmed by the aborigines
Evolving in the folds of the forest
And the forest nestling in the frame of the aborigine
It is you
Who labelled them.

Fear struck
In Jodenghat and Pippaldhari

Indravelli and Babejhari
And in Satnala.*
You wrecked their lives
Shored up with bamboo.

With canisters and cartridges
Mining blood and sulphur gas
You commemorated their baptism
In the seams of the earth.
With all accomplishing
You can never s-lay them again.

3

The valiant emerge
from the very annals they engender.
Can one mark which day
The aborigine was born?
While you brand
20 April year after year
For the current account.
But this time
Staggered by the flash of history
Already on 19 March
You dashed to Devaki's† dungeon.

---

* Jodenghat, Pippaldhari, Indravelli, Babejhari and Satnala are names of
  villages associated with the Adivasi peasant struggle from the 1940s to
  the 1980s.
† Krishna's mother who gave birth to him in prison.

4

The gusty wild-floral wind
Swirls over mountain crests.
The firmament turning the forest (as) sight
Rummages (in) the dust for something.
Unable to see, the Godavari
Shrivels and languishes in bed.

5

People of the day before may be missing yesterday
Yesterday's memorial may have gone today.
Yet, Indravelli prevailed yesterday, today and the day before.

Indravelli may not belong
To the people of the past
Nor could yesterday's Cenotaph own it
But it will not abide by those
Who bulldozed it today.

Nurtured in the flesh and blood of the tribe
The forest will abide
Fused in the primordial vitality
The soul will prevail.
The kiss of the martyrs will persist.

Ganga,* the life current, remains.
Stick and sword will caringly sustain.

---

* In north Telangana, River Godavari is commonly referred to as Ganga.

Even when the whole forest is ransacked
Camouflaged light shimmers and survives.

But, Indravelli
Turned into a town the other day
Will prevail as an emblem of enduring strife.
Yesterday the monument was
A trace of memory.

It will be a millstone for those
Who destroyed it.

Indravelli will hold out
As struggling people's
Peak of vision.

March 1986
Translated by D. Venkat Rao

BESEECHING THE MOTHER

I have never seen that mother
But her index finger points at me.

At times I haven't even seen those children
But the tears of mothers haunt me.

From which soil should I ask her to pick up
Flowers fallen from her lap?
Petals that haven't blossomed yet
Fragrance of those indelible smiles.

How can I suppress this fact:
Those chests that dared bullets
Were harvests of that womb?
The blood spilled on that soil
Was her own milk!
In which eye should I hide my lamentation?
She never aspired to any harvest
But just wanted that crop to flourish.
If not that delicate, affectionate kid,
She could not even see his spilled blood.

She satisfied the hunger of that foetus

---

* 'aa tallimundu dOsiLlatO' from *Muktakantham*, Samudram Prachuranalu, Hyderabad, 1990
  Written after the killing of G. Ramakrishna and V. Nageswara Rao, activists of People's War, in Warangal on 20 May 1986. While Nageswara Rao was a student of the poet, Ramakrishna was an associate in the student movement.

Even before it took shape.
She infused breath into him.
She made him the embodiment of her dreams.
She was the first one to hear
The initial cry of that infant.
Today she doesn't know
In which exile that kid
Let out his last scream
Except in the shock of her warm dream.
Her empty hands could not even experience
The cold touch of her dead child.
Though she was the first
To hug him when he opened his eyes.

You cannot grasp the anguish of that mother today
Unless you understand the labour pains she suffered.

Should I tell that innocent mother
That the children laid down their lives for her?
They sacrificed their lives
For the mother who gave them life!
Should I for that purpose only
Beseech her to contribute more offspring?
Should I seek unending sacrifices
Bowing my head
Before the index finger of that mother?

22 May 1986
Translated by N. Venugopal

CORPSE OF BHETAL

Carrying the dead body from the lock-up on my back
I began walking.
'I will let you know the episode of my death
Solve the riddle: Was it a natural death or murder?'
Said the corpse.

If a dead body, that too from the lock-up, speaks,
That must be a murder
I said.

Despite being happy, as I told the truth
The corpse vanished to be reborn in another lock-up
As it was a crime for a living man to speak.

27–28 September 1986
Translated by N. Venugopal

---

* 'bhEtaaLa Savam' from *Muktakantham,* Samudram Prachuranalu,
Hyderabad,1990
Bhetal is a famous character—a ghost—from the popular Indian folk
story 'Vikram and Bhetal', where Bhetal poses a question every day to
Vikram and vanishes when the latter cannot solve the riddle.

COMPANION

Who keeps me company in these premises?
The blue sky above
Oceans of thoughts within
A shut door and a lock hanging outside
Wide-open memories and the patience I'm so used to, inside.

Are there no human beings here?

This is solitary confinement to my soul.

Trees with fruity minds and flowery hearts
Birds like my urge for freedom
Waiting on the power line
To rise up into the sky.

Other prisoners find time
To stealthily peep in through the crevices of the door.
'Convicts' sneakily wish me
On pretexts of calling me for court or *mulaqat*.[†]

Nobody should meet me
Those around me should not speak with me.

A forced peaceful coexistence
With Congress culture and black marketeers.

---

[*] 'tODu' from *Muktakantham*, Samudram Prachuranalu, Hyderabad, 1990
Written in jail where imprisoned politicians and black marketeers were
the poet's co-prisoners.
[†] A jail jargon for occasionally permitted family visit.

Those speaking with me can't understand my words.
Those who understand can't get my anguish.
The shadow of this block
Is prohibited to fall on the other.

Who is here to keep me company?
A sealed radio and censored newspapers.
If the news of an encounter that is really fake
Is edited out, that is a newspaper.

In the solitary silence of the night
Jailmates from their radio send me
The passion of *Pyaasa** and the agony of *Malliswari.*†
Stars tossed in packets of jasmine
(They get stones in marijuana packets from the street outside).

If you tune into the radio for news here
You find only . . . death.

Death-fang on life's struggle
A forced end to the dreams of the youth.
Waiting is the only company
To the tears that swirl in me.
Elongated, sleepless nights,
Sound of tracks in the books
That run on my tongue.
It isn't noise from the fan
But the outrage of waterfalls within my mind.

---

* A famous 1957 Hindi film by Guru Dutt.
† A famous 1951 Telugu film by B.N. Reddy.

Black letters turn into red blood cells,
They enter me and give me renewed strength.

As a person who's slept amidst rails
After intense running
I wake up with broken nightmares.

As emotion runs high
My mind in teary thoughts
Beats *Choma's Drum.**
I imagine the phoenix
Turning to ashes in the peace of a graveyard.

In the movement
Between dawn and dusk
Who keeps me company?
Foresight supplies breath
The mind believes in spring thunder.

17 September 1986
Translated by N. Venugopal

---

* The disturbing drumbeat by the main character Choma in the 1975
Kannada film *Chomana Dudi*, based on Shivarama Karanth's novel of the
same name.

DÉJÀ VU

Lucky
You are born rich.
As you say in your lingo
'Born with a silver spoon in the mouth'.

Your agitation sounds creative
Our agony appears violent.

You are meritorious
You can break the windows of buses
In a shape as symmetric as the sun's rays.

You can deflate the tyres
With artistic elan
While indulgent police look on
Their jaws nestling on rifle butts.

You can tie rakhis
Even in the dark chambers
Of a police station.
You do not buy a bus ticket
Not because your pocket is empty
That is your genuine protest.

---

* 'Dajaavu' from *Muktakantham*, Samudram Prachuranalu, Hyderabad, 1990
  Much before the country-wide anti-Mandal agitation of 1989, a similar
  agitation was led by upper-class, upper-caste youths of Andhra Pradesh
  in 1986 against a state-level commission's recommendation for increase
  in reservations.

The beautiful roads
Are all yours
Whether you do a *rastaroko**
Or drive vehicles with 'Save Merit'† stickers.

Barefeet, we reek of sweat
What if we built the roads?
The meritorious plan is yours.
The credit of contract is also yours.

Those exhilarating sixty days.
What fun!
When your cute little girls
And their daredevil mates
Were going on a delectable rampage . . .

Everybody was delighted
Parents, their parents
Brothers and sisters
Even the servants.
Newspapers?
Oh, absolutely thrilled!

Boys and girls
Protesting hand in hand
Against buried merits and dashed futures
Going off on a picnic

---

* Blockade of road.
† The agitations against protective discrimination policy always allege that the policy kills merit, and raise this slogan.

Oh *yaar*,*
How heroic!

You are the marathoners
In merit competition.
Poor tortoises,
Can we run with you?

If you serve tea in Chikkadpalli
Sell peanuts in a cinema hall
Polish boots in Kothi Circle
Stop a Maruti or Priya† on the Tankbund‡
To demand agitation fund.

Media persons are 'merit' creatures
Their camera hearts 'click'
Their pens shriek
'Youthful brilliance!'

We are drab-faced duds
Sitting in the stink of dead animals.
We make shoes
Applying colour with our blood
And polishing them
With the sinking light of our eyes.

However
Isn't the shine different

---

* A colloquial Hindi/Urdu word for associate.
† Maruti and Priya are brands of four-wheelers and two-wheelers, respectively.
‡ Chikkadpalli, Kothi Circle and Tankbund are places in Hyderabad.

When polished
By someone in boots?

We clean up your filth
Carry the nightsoil on our heads.
We wear out our bodies
Washing your rooms
To make them sparkle
Like your scented bodies.

We sweep, we clean.
Our hands are brooms.
Our sweat is water.
Our blood is the phenyl.
Our bones are washing powder.
But all this
Is menial labour.
What merit it has?
What skill?

If you sweep
The cement road with a smile
Tucked-in shirts and miniskirts
Jeans and high heels
It becomes an Akashvani scoop
And spellbinding Doordarshan*spectacle.

We are
Rickshaw pullers
Porters and hawkers
Petty shopkeepers

---

* Akashvani and Doordarshan are popular media outlets run by the
government.

And low-grade clerks.

We are
Desolate mothers
Who can give no milk
To the child who bites in hunger.

We stand in hospital queues
To sell blood to buy food.
Except
For the smell of poverty and hunger
How can it acquire
The patriotic flavour
Of your blood donation?

Whatever you do
Sweep or polish
Carry luggage in a railway station
Or in a bus stand
Vend fruits on a pushcart
Sell chai on a footpath
Take out a procession
With 'Save merit' placards

We know
It is to show us that
Our laborious professions
Are no match to your merit.

White coats and black badges
Hanging over chiffon sarees and Punjabi dresses.*

_____

* A particular young female attire from Punjab, popular all over the country
  and a symbol of modernism.

'Save merit' stickers on your chests
carrying stethoscopes.
When you walk in front of the *daftar**
Even heaven is aflutter
For the poor among you
And those who crossed the 12000[†] among us
The reservation G.O.[‡]
Is not only a dream shattered and heaven shaken
But also a rainbow broken.

Yours
Is a movement for justice
On this earthly paradise.
That is why
'*Devathas*'[§] dare more for the sacred nectar.

The moment
You gave a call for '*jail bharo*'[¶]
We were shifted out
From the barracks
To rotting dungeons.
A great welcome was prepared
Red carpets were spread.
('Red' only in idiom
The colour scares
even those who spread it.)

---

* Office.
[†] While reservations were accorded to people from 'forward castes', also known as Economically Backward Classes, it is restricted to the families whose annual income was less than Rs 12,000.
[‡] A government order.
[§] Angels.
[¶] Fill the jails, a form of protest.

We waited with fond hope for the pious dust of your feet
To grace not only the country
But its jails too.

How foolish!
The meritorious cream
The future
Of the country's glorious dream
How can they come
To the hell of thieves,
Murderers and subversives?

We read and rejoice
That function halls
Where rich marriages are celebrated
Became your jails.

Ours may be a lifelong struggle till death
But yours is a rich wedding party.
If you show displeasure
It is like a marriage tiff.
If you burn furniture
It is pyrotechnical stuff.
If you observe *bandh**
It is the landlord's daughter's marriage.

Lucky
The corpse of your merit
Parades through the main streets

---

* Strike, stoppage of every social activity.

Has its funeral at the crossroads
Amid chanting of holy mantras.

But Merit has no death
So you creatively conduct a symbolic procession
And enact the mourning.
In us
To die or to be killed
There is no merit.

We die
With hunger or disease
Doing hard labour or committing crime
In lock-up or encounter.
(The Meritorious will not agree that inequality is violence.)

We will be thrown
By a roadside
In a filthy pit
On a dust heap
In a dark forest.

We will turn to ash
Without a trace.
We will go missing
From a hill or a hole.

Our births and deaths
Become census statistics.
What other use do they have
For national progress?

We take birth
And perish
Live and die in
Miserable poverty.
You assume avatars
when Dharma is in danger
And renounce that role
After completing the job.
You are the *sutradhar*.*

You are lucky.
You are meritorious.

October 1986
Translated by K. Balagopal

---

* In Sanskrit drama, the person who conducts the show.

PARADISE OF LOVE

Nobody could divide us.

What are we, after all?
Soil and man
Us and the multitude.

Between us
If you are a garden, I am the breeze.
If you are a fort, I am the flag.
You are the city
And I am your artery and pulse.
Now I am your restless heatwave in exile.
I am a piece of the monolith[†]
That sings about wounds of togetherness
In this separation.

Oh, the city that taught me
Even as it learnt from me.
The city that spread my words
While teaching me how to talk.
The city that paved my path

---

* 'prEmanagar' from *Muktakantam*, Samudram Prachuranalu, Hyderabad, 1990
  The poem is an ode to Warangal, a town in north Telangana, where the poet was educated from middle school until his graduation. He also worked as a lecturer and activist in the town for over three decades.
† Warangal, the town with which the poet is emotionally attached, derived its name after a huge monolith. The capital city of a medieval empire was built around the monolith during the eleventh century.

While making me sing.
The city that loved me and
Was enamoured in my love.
Oh, my gift and my curse
My first love
My Paradise Lost . . .
Can I ever regain you?

I haven't spent as much time
With my mother or in my native village
Or even with my better half
Or with my kids
As I spent with you.

Your water flows in my blood.
I am at home in this water.
Your wind inspires my breath.
I cannot stand any other air.
Each morsel in my food is from your lap.
You are everything to me.
You are the axis to my cart.

As my friend from afar teases me
You are Telangana.
As we describe you
You are the North Telangana struggle.
Now you are the anguish
Filled in my imagination.

When our people marched in the movement
The days we walked hand in hand
The roads we washed with our tears

The path of our people's sacrifices.
The times when we listened to the legends of
Our adventures with bated breath.

Today whatever I hear about you
It is like holding yesterday's
Heart on the palm and listening to it.

When you tell our history
It is like reliving our memories.
As you move on with our works
I feel as if my feet walk along with you.

Your march will not stop
But, please, without diverting your attention
Call me once, can't you?
The call that injects oxygen into me
The call that was kindled by my breath
The call that makes me restless.

27 June 1987
Translated by N. Venugopal

THE DEATH OF A HUMAN

The death of a human unsettles me.

Call him a martyr or say that
he turned into a star.
Humanity is gagged
Nevertheless when a human dies.

No one knows where he comes from
No one knows his name, and there's
No one he is related to, but
The murderer knows well that
The one who dies is human.

The tree that sprinkles flowers
In the form of tears knows.
The wind that blows a fistful of soil
Upon the dead body knows.

A human is a fragment in the puzzle of society
He is never alone. He is made of sunlight
Moisture from the ocean and soil.
When the torch of life is put out,
The heart turns dark.

I may have not known him before
Or ever heard his name

---

* 'manishi maraNam' from *Muktakantham*, Samudram Prachuranalu, Hyderabad, 1990

Had I seen his face in any photo
I wouldn't even recognize him.
But when I know that he is human too
How can I not be related to him?

May 1987
Translated by Rohith

SUPERNOVA

As the light of the sun or the moon
Fills the earth, how many histories
Of stars does the darkness mask
How many rays of light escape
The entrails of darkness, how many
Luminous streams fall prey to the
Cravings of a galaxy?
The story of a star's
Explosion has to travel lakhs of light years
To reach us, and in the present
In the place of a star that has long died
All we see is a fledgling star being born.

7 July 1987
Translated by Rohith

---

* 'sooparnOvaa' from *Muktakantham,* Samudram Prachuranalu, Hyderabad,
1990

THE DREAM PIGEONS

Pigeons released by heart
Alight on the eyelids.
You know I am scared to open
My eyes and break the wings
And so, I pretend, with my eyes closed.

I know very well that my
Dreams are not my creations alone
And that imagination is not
Anyone's secret.

10 August 1987
Translated by Rohith

---

* 'kalala paavuraalu' from *Muktakantham*, Samudram Prachuranalu, Hyderabad, 1990

CHUNRI

She is only a kid.
Should we ask her?
No, we did not, not at her wedding.
She was given to a royal house
Married with such pomp.
Old and young, friends and neighbours
So many people came.

She cried while going to her in-laws' house
All of us wept too.
But, was it really dislike?
It was only habitual affection.

2

That day
When we were giving her a bath
She said she was afraid.
It was only fear of the unknown, we assured her.
She insisted that she would sleep with her mother or sister
We forced sense into her mind.

---

* 'chunree' from *Muktakantham*, Samudram Prachuranalu, Hyderabad,
  1990
  The poem was written in the context of a nationwide protest against the
  burning of an eighteen-year-old widow, Roop Kanwar, on her husband's
  pyre in Rajasthan in September 1987, as per the Hindu–Rajput tradition
  of Sati. Chunri is a veil all married women had to wear in some north-
  Indian states.

Afraid, she refused to go into
That dim-lit room.
With the fumes of incense and perfume of camphor
She did not budge from the door.
We pushed her in and bolted it.

Should we allow her out?
Even if she shouted or knocked at the door?
We spent a whole night there with jokes and laughter.

But, tell me if this is use of force?

3

We said the same thing that day
When she was crying on his dead body.
Once again we made her a bride.
She went on to the sandal pyre
That smelled of burning ghee*
With a jar in her hands
As she had gone into the nuptial room
With a milk tumbler in her hands.†

Her husband's head on her lap
We don't know whether she cried or laughed
But that was drowned in our
'*Sati Mata ki jai*'‡ slogans.

---

* Saturated butter, used to light fire on the pyre.
† Traditionally a wife would be sent into the nuptial bedroom on the ceremonial first night with a milk tumbler in her hands.
‡ A slogan in Hindi hailing the custom of bride burning and adoring her as a mother figure.

Intoxicated with the scenes that
We imagined outside the bedroom
On that nuptial night
We lost ourselves amidst the armed guard.

Swear on that smiling appearance
And tell me please
Was it murder?

4

It is true that
He dragged her on to his pyre
As he would drag her on to his bed
With the same authority.

She performed sati as freely
As she lived.

12 October 1987
Translated by N. Venugopal

POETRY

Poetry is truth that need not be concealed
People who do not need government
Life that doesn't need ambrosia

If you search my pockets
Ransack the books and papers on my table
And the racks on the shelves
Pry open my flower-like ribcage
There is no secret other than poetry.

My dangerous personality
That you do not understand:
The secret is poetry.

Look carefully
It is like moonlight trapped in a rectangle.
In an arrogant pose
You look up to insult me.

See, my poetry shines in the blue sky as a full moon
You see the moon and are shocked
But surprisingly the moon cannot see itself in this cell.

I used to feel disgusted
When you used to comb through my body.
Now

---

* 'kavitvam' from *Muktakantham*, Samudram Prachuranalu, Hyderabad, 1990

After I poured out all my blood
And transfused it with poetry
To be my companion in solitude
I pity you as I treat your search in my lap
As a search for your lost humanity.
When you grope around my neck
Your metal detector trembles on my chest.
I surrender myself to you
As if I am exploring my own secret worlds
Uncovering myself and peeling my own skin
To hear my own poetic voice
To feel the attraction of touch
In your hands that shackle me.
Poetry descends like a heavy weight
As you attach a chain.
Whenever I move
Noise of soaring free birds.

In the daylight of court
Prosecution conspiracies come out.

You go on about surveillance
Poetry gets ignited and continues to fire.
You go on about governance
Poetry talks about people even in sleep.
You throw the net of death and keep waiting
Poetry swims in consciousness just before your eyes.

Poetry is an open secret—the state ceases to exist
As poetry takes shape in my heart.
It reaches those it has to . . .
Even as it rises in my imagination

It inspires people to act in unison.
The secret is that
My poetry took birth
With the first signs of people's struggles.

My poetry
Continues to flow like a blood letter stream
Out of your hands that closed mine
Like a broken string of pain and thread of anger
Like the sight that lights tears.

30 December 1987
Translated by N. Venugopal

'NO CLASSES TOMORROW'

Those kids helplessly stand
At the zebra crossing on the road
The hurry to hang on to their moms' necks filling their eyes.

The weight of homework on their backs pulls down their neck
Hair like fallen petals of withered flowers
Uniforms that drain all the colour in their face
Shoes that stop the mercuric feet running before time.

In the midst of an urban forest
Those kids are listless visions of
Fallen stars.

Vehicles stop only for the red signal
But not for the kids.

The hands that turn the wheel
That manage the handle and apply brakes
All the hands otherwise embrace those kids
But now, no one looks at them.

I waved at them with affection
But they looked at my hand strangely

---

* 'rEpu klaasulu lEvu' from *Muktakantham*, Samudram Prachuranalu, Hyderabad, 1990
  A scene at a crossroads near the Secretariat in the city, seen from the escort police van when the poet was being brought back to jail from court.

As if thinking
What is this melody amidst this din?
Recognizing the smile from within the police van
They sniffed a message in my handcuffed and raised fist
'Tomorrow there won't be any classes.'

As they cross the road noisily
The vehicles stopped
Like stones in the stream.
The children ran with wild joy
Without looking back.

5 February 1988
Translated by N. Venugopal

WORDS

Words, smothered in the folds of the self
Must be stirred awake
Made to trot and watch
See if the wings can bear aloft
The crippled limbs
And soar into the sky.

Like the first showers after a drought
To my parched ears, my own words
Not another's, remain strange.

Like the marvel of the sky
Discovering its lost monsoon
I long to sprout on a soil
In the vibrations of a sonorous world.

Once again I yearn to learn the utterance
At school and on the commune
From pupils and plebians
I dream of seizing syllables
From each of history's furrows.

Without this resounding peal
How will this silence
Loaded for so long in the self
Explode?

---

* 'maaTalu' from *Muktakantham*, Samudram Prachuranalu, Hyderabad,
1990

Without this booming resonance
How will this scene
Crypted for so long in the eyes
Scintillate?

Once again I must learn to utter
In communing with and listening
Our people.
I must be tethered to the word, abide by it.
What's one's legacy after betraying the word?

Nothing debases the word:
In the blazing furnaces of time
Under the plummeting hammer clangs
This, as the fittest moment
I go on forging expressions.

March 1988
Translated by D. Venkat Rao

AFTER ALL YOU SAY

For me
The scene of writing
Torsioning out word-chains,
From the seams of the earth
An endless movement.

In writing too
Pressure and stress inflexing soundings
In a weave of interanimation
Force regendering
Words
Insurge as frontlines.

My self seems
Inscribed.
Forces that lived in me
Awaiting future lives.

The blood
On the sweat-smelling
Person's forehead is indelible.
I try and mop it
I can neither touch nor soil
The glorious sunscape stretched into the stellar space.

---

* 'nuvventa cheppoo' from *Muktakantham*, Samudram Prachuranalu, Hyderabad, 1990
  Written in jail in response to a letter from a friend discussing his voracious reading while in prison.

As I pore over
The work in my hands
It moves me into the hands
That are in the work.
Unknowingly moving into them
I spread the work
On my self.
It is indeed a feeling beyond compare!
Reading in silence
I feel unblinking looks
My tongue plays while my lips move
As the vital chords of myself
Reverberate encompassing gong waves.

I feel
As if the work
Has uttered in me the clues
To this (s)cryptic universe.
Yet I know
This is only empathy
And that I haven't lived through the work.

I am shaking awake
The multitudes to encounter from my bones:
Taming the volcanoes
And tending the spring-currents
From the innards of my earth-self
Perhaps like Pavlov's dog.

But for me
Used to reading man as a text

Can the book become a substitute
For the world?

July 1988
Translated by D. Venkat Rao

MEGHYA

A single drop of your blood, if shed
Might blossom, a raindrop, they feared.

The many blows left no trace
Hardening you, your body a shock to the system
Your body hung
A portent at the crossroads.

Freedom-loving birds
Offering withered blades of grass
To scarecrows
Located the man in the corpse
The rebel within.

All summers are not alike.
For desert-lives, an oasis appears
Somewhere . . .
Languishing under a long summer
A flash of thunder is enough
For the dry branch—shaded by this date palm—
To flower again.

Like clouds hiding thunder
In their hearts
People preserved your memories
Became a storm

* 'mEghyaa' from *Unnadedo Unnattu*, Viplava Rachayitala Sangham, Hyderabad, 2000

A thunderous roar
A sea churning.

You became a perennial stream
Earth-bound, a rising spring.

Summer gets hotter each year
No trace of a tree nearby
No taste of water for parched throats.
All along the road
Only trenches, truncated paths, topless manholes
Horrendous horns, oil-spills
Sudden breaks, riding shotgun
Brazen sirens, fear-sweats, road rollers
Lathis, tear gas, bullets
Torn chappals, the miasma of a daily routine.
In the fierce summer in the city
You are like a victory post
Planted three years ago.

Meghya, you flow in a cool torrent
Jetting along, a cool relief
You offer a soothing touch
To the heart.

The soil under the feet is wet too
With memories
As it unfolds
In yet another
Adventure.

May 1993
Translated by K. Damodar Rao

HUMAN BEING WITH A VOICE

Hidden in thick mango foliage
The cuckoo sings of the coming
Of spring.

The peacock with its thousand-eyed feathers
Dances in pleasure at the onset of rain
In the darkness of the forest.

The blue jay vanishes in the sky
While people march, heralding
The arrival of the right time
For taking arms from the jammi tree.

Birds in the forest
Make agitated noises
To alert the grazing cattle and the jumping calf
About the pouncing tiger.

Waves inform the fish in water
About the imminent net.
Rough weather tells the pigeon in the nest
About the preying snare.

Who then will tell good and bad
To that person who does not have voice

---

* 'nOrunna manishi' from *Unnadedo Unnattu*, Viplava Rachayitala Sangham,
Hyderabad, 2000

Who only has two hands that work
And a stomach?

10 December 1997

Translated by N. Venugopal

ONLY WORK WE ARE CAPABLE OF

To offer subsidized gas cylinders
After putting an end to subsidized rice
Is an art.

To offer the *deepam* to women
After extinguishing the light of the house
Is an art.

To announce the *janmabhoomi* scheme
After deploying police in the lands of tillers
Is also an art.

We believe
Acting is an art
Eulogy is poetry.

We extol a comprador
Who mortgaged our self-respect

---

* 'manaku chEtanaina pani' from *Unnadedo Unnattu*, Viplava Rachayitala
Sangham, Hyderabad, 2000
This poem refers to populist schemes announced by the then chief
minister of Andhra Pradesh N. Chandrababu Naidu even as he stopped
the existing scheme of subsidized rice and introduced several policies
recommended by the World Bank in its 'Agenda for Economic Reforms:
Andhra Pradesh'. He announced the Deepam scheme for subsidized
gas cylinder for rural women, and brought in the Janmabhoomi scheme
of land reforms, which did not include a land distribution scheme but
imposed restrictions on land struggles, such as imposing Sec. 144 and
Sec. 30 in villages and fields, arresting peasants and landless labourers
under the TADA, prohibiting meetings, etc.

To get World Bank loans
We call him Telugu self-pride.

Yes, we are intellectuals
That is the only work we are capable of.

3 August 1999
Translated by N. Venugopal

STORY OF SEVEN SISTERS
AS TOLD BY A LITTLE FINGER

Seven sisters went to collect flowers.
They had to go deep into the forest
As a serpentine road encircled the Godavari
And all the flower and fruit trees were lost.

Adolescents all of them
They were
Flowers that blossomed halfway.

From Korutla, Metpalli and Jagityal,† Bombay and Dubai have
    become nearer
For food or livelihood.
On the canal-like roads
You get cassettes but not flowers.
Anyway we cannot go to Amsterdam
For our own flowers.

---

* 'tegipaDina chiTikenavElu . . .' from *Unnadedo Unnattu*, Viplava
  Rachayitala Sangham, Hyderabad, 2000
  The poem is a response to the news of seven teenage girls killed on
  the banks of the Godavari. The poet alludes to a popular folk song in
  Telangana, in which seven sisters go to a forest to collect flowers and
  firewood, and a tiger devours them all. A folk singer finds the little finger
  of one of the girls fallen on the ground and puts it in his basket. The
  surviving finger comes alive to tell the story of the sisters.
† Korutla, Metpalli, Jagityal are names of towns in Karimnagar district,
  from where a lot of migration to Mumbai and the Gulf countries takes
  place by working class people in search of livelihood.

That's why those kids of Manthani*
Scarlet flowers themselves
Went to the forest for flowers.

Nearing the age of marriage and the age of promises
They were not alone, they were
Collecting flowers of their choice
Picking stones in the stream and taking baths.

Rice was cooking on the bank under the tree.
They had time and passion
To play in the stream till the rice was cooked.

The smell and sound of cooking rice
The feel and sparkle of running water
The raging dreams of seven youngsters
Jumping from childhood into adolescence.

Not that they don't know about the wild animals.
In fact the animals give way to the activists.

Now it should be hyenas on the highway
Hounds that pounce on the herd
Greyhounds arrive from the other side
Diverting the attention of the sentry on the road.

Now
The splashing of water is not there
Not even the sound of fingers that collect flowers
Except the rancour of wolves.

---

* A town in Karimnagar district.

Everything that is sensitive is destroyed.

Girls bright like early sunlight on the flowing waters
Now in blood-spattered pieces
Boiling rice thrown into dust.

When the crescents were cut
The blood flowed frozen
The embarrassed forest darkened.

The girls who went for flowers
Came back as mutilated dreams.

Seeing the bare dead bodies of their flower-like children
Their mothers' tears not only screamed
But raged as well.

2000

Translated by N. Venugopal

ONLY TO DEMOLISH

Not as constricted as a house
The doll house that kids make
Does not have walls
It's only a nest of birds
Hanging from a branch like a bunch of flowers.

In the sandy bed of a stream
Children themselves become one with nature
To build a nest around their feet
And boisterously clap
If water washes it out
And celebrate sand turning
Into stream.

They make a paper boat or a knife boat
That may drown or flow away
With the weight of flowers.
They wait in anxious exuberance
To see the boats unite at the horizon.

But then
Where are the sandy streams?
Where are the nests?
Where are the boats and strolls?

---

* 'koolchaDaanikE' from *Antassootram,* Nayanodya Prachuranalu,
Hyderabad, 2006
Written in prison, when the poet heard that his three-year-old grandson,
Aman, was building a doll house, with a specific provision for a jail room
for his grandfather, who had been imprisoned for his writings.

Even walls have become
The shadows of apartments
With only corridors outside the walls
Without air and without light
Balconies have grills and security
But no amaranths
And not even bougainvillea.

Just ask the kids
What does nature mean to them?
It is only the artificial stars
On the dark ceiling of their bedroom!

All kids in the world
Very well know that
They get beaten up
If they are insistent.

Now, they are coming to know
That they would be sent to jail
If they speak.

Now, in the doll houses they build
They are learning to make provision
For a jail room for the grandpa who writes poetry.

But they build the prison house
Only to demolish.

17 January 2006
Translated by N. Venugopal

TO TEACH KIDS 1

Today's little ones,
Are beaten up, shouted at
And lied to.

That's how they are trained to be
Tomorrow's citizens of this country.

When they grow up
They will repeat what they were taught
Some of them from positions of power
Most of them downtrodden.

TO TEACH KIDS 2

Kids, when they are still little
Smudge their clothes as they
Play in the mud, like a worker
From the coal mine who digs up
And carries loads.

They are dragged back
To tailored uniforms, sent to school

---

* 'biDDalaSikshaNa' from Antassootram, Nayanodaya Prachuranalu,
  Hyderabad, 2006

And disciplined.

It is only then
They grow up to be
Army generals and
Receive medals for chivalry.

18 January 2006
Translated by Rohith

SCHOOLS AND PRISONS

It is to chain freedom
That a school or a prison exists.

They are the centres of 'reform'
To train kids to be adults
To make criminals out of humans.

It is only until they don't speak up
They are 'cute'.
It is only if they walk
There are barriers.

To deprive kids of their 'mother tongue' and to imbibe the
Language of 'authorities'
They are sent to schools.

Those who speak of humanity in this system
Are thrown into prison to acquaint them
With the vocabulary of 'criminology'.

Kids are admonished
When they turn too mischievous
And adults are clamped down
On the pretext of becoming 'outrageous'.

---

* 'skoolu – jailu' from *Antassootram*, Nayanodaya Prachuranalu, Hyderabad,
2006

At home, when parents fight
It's like the ruling party and the opposition
Arguing.
But when it comes to sending
Kids to school or prison
They get together and pass resolutions
Like a unanimous decision in the parliament.

Education is to learn obedience
From pre-school
To pre-university
That's how they come to lie enough
To get qualified to be rulers.

Prisoners are those who commit crime
Against private property
And the system calls them 'unlawful'.
Unless they turn malevolent
They are all humans like us.

Though, no matter how many generations
Of children turn old,
There are always new children.

2 February 2006
Translated by Rohith

THE WIND IN MECCA MASJID

The wind in Mecca Masjid
Knows the force of little children's hands
That throw jowar grains for pigeons.
It knows the strength in the wings of descending pigeons.
It also knows the light in the eyes of boisterous kids.
Yes, it knows the mutter of the pigeons swimming in the pool.

The wind around Mecca Masjid knows
The old lady selling grains for the pigeons
Jaffer Mian offering guavas to feed the pigeons
The echo of their toil going waste.
It knows the twittering of the kids' dreams
Growing wings under the shadow of the masjid.

It also knows the raucous silence amidst the lone sound of azan
Thousands of voices calling Allah all the time.

The wind came there for
Respite after heavy pounding
Under the hi-tech wheels of Greater Hyderabad.

---

* 'makkaa maseedu gaali' from *Varavara Rao Kavitvam 1957–2017*,
Swechchasahiti, Hyderabad, 2017
This poem is a response to the blasts at Hyderabad's 400-year-old Mecca
Masjid on 18 May 2007. At least thirteen people were killed in the blasts
and the violence that followed, when police opened fire to control a mob
(https://indianexpress.com/article/what-is/mecca-masjid-blast-2007-
hyderabad-nia-aseemanand-5139063/;
https://www.thehindu.com/news/cities/Hyderabad/intervention-in-
mecca-masjid-blast-case-sought/article65427343.ece).

The wind doesn't know only one thing
That a blare can turn jowar grains into poison,
Send terrified pigeons fluttering
Take the life breath of the little ones
Without even giving a moment to shake off the smiles
Makes the grain basket of *ammijaan* a lap of blood
And lets off a venomous snake from the guava that bites Jaffer Mian.

The wind that blows through Mecca Masjid's domes
Has never ever heard the din of a remote-control destruction.

The wind knows what it is to flow invisibly
But it doesn't know invisible plots.

For a long time the wind knew
Police guards are there to protect petrodollars
From fakirs and the unemployed
From believers of the green crescent in the blue sky
From a nation that lost the land under its feet.

The Mecca Masjid wind knows all of them since their birth
Those who lost their lives
In the RDX blasts
To the police rubber bullets
Whether they are children or aged
All of them were born and brought up on the soil
Where that wind blows.
It also knows that they are Muslims
Since they come there at regular intervals.

It only doesn't know
That some of them die

Due to 'foreign conspiracy'
And some
Die to the rubber bullets fired by police
To protect lives of people.

Yesterday after *johar* also
After the blasts and police firing
The wind greeting everybody as usual
Touched the bodies of the fallen
And smoothly closed their eyelids
Understood the life desire in their hearts and moved on.

Not only at dawn
But also at dusk
Fingers turn wind into song from the holes of *shehanai*,
The same fingers that write grains for pigeons.

2007
Translated by N. Venugopal

WHAT WE NEED IS POETRY

The poetry
Of tears, of dreams, of enchantments
Poetry of memories and futilities
Poetry of hope, dashed hopes
Aspirations, experiences and emotions.

The poetry with an embryo
That explodes into a blossom
The poetry that flowers
Releases fragrance and
Comes to fruition.

The poetry with a spine
That can stand up to the system
And hold it accountable,
The poetry that refuses power
The poetry that challenges the state.

The poetry with a vision
A foresight and an eye
On the ground.
The poetry of the smile of an infant
That spreads like love, motherly poetry.

The poetry that won't shy away from disdain,
The poetry that can bring a world of affection

---

* 'kavitvam kaavaali' from *Beejabhoomi,* Viplava Rachayitala Sangham, Hyderabad, 2014

To its reader.

The poetry that's as much a synonym to
Melancholy as it is to solace
The poetry that can stand
On either side of the proletariat
The poetry that paves the way
For the workers' tomorrow.

The poetry that's churned out
Of the immensity of existence
The poetry that's a symbol
Of the ocean of abysmal lives.

The poetry that's a metaphor of our fights
And another world
The poetry of democracy
The poetry of people's struggles.

31 January 2013
Translated by Rohith

GOODBYE

For me it's just a walk out
Leaving everything
All that confidence
All those utterances
All those boasts
All the cooing pigeons
In Chanchalguda Jail,[†]
All that dirt and blood
Under the bridge
Insults, hatred, curfews
Tears and pleasures
Friendships and affections
Fears and courage
Jealousy, wrath and warmth.

I can leave
The shadow of Chaderghat Police Station
Nalgonda Cross Roads bus stop
Ceaseless conversations of the dumb
Blind girls touching the shreds of the bomb
With their tears to clear
Fragmented dead bodies of Palestinian kids.
The regular hungry beggar

---

* 'alvidaa' from *Beejabhoomi,* Viplava Rachayitala Sangham, Hyderabad,
  2014
  Written at the time of shifting a house after more than twenty years.
† A central jail in which the poet was lodged for several years. The jail is
  quite close to Nalgonda Cross Roads, where the poet resided.

The fakir who says *allah-ke-naam** without accepting any alms
The evening traffic jams
Amidst the perfumes of jasmine bunches
Selling on Chaderghat† lower bridge covering the Musi's stink
Neighbours and pleasures and pains
Unceasing supports, embraces and hugs.

Not until I left everything in Nalgonda Cross Roads
Did I realize
I can never erase the blood stain of his tears
Drenching my arm when he hugged me farewell.
I can never become a sigh
Of her restrained tears and breath.

23 July 2014
Translated by N. Venugopal

---

* A poetic refrain of Sufi alms seekers singing on the streets.
† A bridge on the river Musi where flowers are sold, in contrast to the stinking gutter the river below has turned into.

FIRE IS JUSTICE

When I was a kid
My mother told me a story:

Each individual holds fire in their heart
Like the hearth in front of the house
And the fireplace in the kitchen.

Fire lies in the womb of the shami tree[†]
Amidst jowar fields
Symbol of social justice for all villagers.
When injustice spreads in the village and world
When it becomes intolerable
All villagers march towards the tree
To take justice back into their hands.
That is the time the jay on the jowar stack
Greets us flying in the sky
Like a fluttering flag against the blue.

Yes, there is fire hidden in every tree
In the hands or branches or green leaves
Or the pollen of the flowers
Or in the roots underneath.

---

[*] 'nippu manishi kanipeTTina nyaayam' from *Beejabhoomi*, Viplava
Rachayitala Sangham, Hyderabad, 2014
[†] Shami tree is the place where the Pandavas stored their weapons before
going on exile, to be redeemed when it was time for war. Thus, shami is a
symbol of revival of war. In Telangana, on the day of Dussehra, villagers
go to a shami tree to pay respects. People customarily hold jowar stacks
during this procession. The appearance of a jay bird is seen as a good
omen for victory.

Only wind has to bring those hands together
That's enough
Like a possessed village goddess
A whirlwind rages
And the forest gets torched.
Otherwise, how do you explain forest fires?

There is fire even in stone that is supposed to be lifeless
Haven't humans discovered fire from the friction of stones?

Hands should always spread light
Like flintstones in front of our eyes.
Vision should always sparkle
From behind the eyelids like fireflies.

Doesn't the firefly always keep a flame
Under its wings?

The tears in the eyes of returning men
After immersing *pirs*
The fire that is generated on the palms
Of the *dhula** players is a common invocation.

When the planet earth itself is a broken part of sun
All people on this earth ought to be walking fires.

Fires should never extinguish
Humans should never smother.

---

* In Telangana villages, Muharram is observed by both Muslims and Hindus, who dance around fire, *alava*, and this dance form is known as *dhula*. As Muharram is an occasion of remembrance of sacrifice, people cry during the immersion of *pirs*. Here, the poet is taking the unity of tears and fire as a metaphor.

Health is measured in
Temperature, pulse and heartbeat.
The heart's raging fire is the light in the eyes
Fire has to go on sprouting in the heart's moisture.

10 December 2014
Translated by N. Venugopal

HOMECOMING

That sixteen-year-old boy, well versed in Quran
Has become the protector of his parents
Even before attaining adulthood.

As the Jama Masjid imam announced
The sight of Ramadan moon
He went to Delhi on Eid
To buy new clothes and chute-ki-semiya.

He was innocent
He didn't know
Muslims have no place
Even in trains in this country.

Eager to be together on this festive day
His father rushed to the station
To find his son, blood-soaked,
A dead body, a hacked new moon.

The mother does not know
Why everybody in the village
Throws agonized looks at her.

Why everybody mentions her grown-up son
As a memory of the past.

---

* 'gharvaapasee' from *Varavara Rao Kavitvam 1957–2017,* Swechchasahiti,
  Hyderabad, 2017

On the corpse of her son
Who promised to come back before sunset
She finds new clothes filled with bloodstains
Daggers that pierce the heart of the mother.

In the evening sky of this country
There is space only for the moon on *chaviti*
But the new moon is prohibited.

They remove and throw away
The skull caps from the heads
As they would sever heads from torsos
They pull beards, blame mullahs.

To say they acted like beasts,
Charging at others for the crime of eating beef
Is indeed an insult to beasts.

How can a believer
Become an anti-national?

We know blood turns into sweat and
Yields crops, becomes scent
Transforms into thousands of occupations.
We know how blood turns into milk
And springs out as motherly affection.

Now we came to experience
The fanatical hatred that takes out
Blood from a tender infant.

One country under the same sky
An arena of divisive hatred

Dost,
Can't there be Home Coming*
Do we have only Ghar Wapsi?

2017
Translated by N. Venugopal

---

* Home Coming refers to the Biblical promise of Jesus. It is also the title
of a book of literary criticism by Kenyan writer Ngugi wa Thiong'o. It is
also famous as Yasser Arafat's 1994 address to Palestinians.

A RIVER BORN IN NASIK

Since the first spring
The river is witnessing
Human beings struggling in sludge on its banks
Collecting roots and tubers
Making tools out of stone melting their own muscle
Inventing fire, hunting, singing and dancing
Drenching soil with their blood and sweat.
The river also saw them diverting its own self
To harvest crops
With lifts, canals, drawing wheels and reservoirs
It saw farmers creating a glorious world
Adding a little water, a little dew
A little sunlight and a little air
More of their flesh and blood
To adorn soil with magical powers.

When the market entered the farmer's life
For the selfish motive of the 'invisible hand'
The river saw everybody from
The commission agent to the broker getting rich
As farmers remained forever in debt.

Everybody paid lip service and announced their debt to the farmer
But the farmer is the only one who doesn't enjoy loan waiver

---

* 'naasiklO puTTina gOdaavari' published in *Andhra Jyoti* literary
supplement, 19 March 2018
Written after the historic peasant march from Nashik to Mumbai, a
180-km-long march, undertaken by about 40,000 farmers between 6–12
March 2018.

The farmer does not get remunerative prices and warehouses
Banks that cherish serving the Mallyas and Modis*
Turn barren cows for farmers.
As the idiom goes, for a farmer it is a forest to sell and a fire to buy.

The farmer alone doesn't know the value of labour.
The river wondered what was greater
The water it carried
Or the tears and blood of farmers
In peasant struggles or farmers' suicides.

The river expressed its fury
Accompanied by the forest
It changed its direction
And marched to the capital.
In the land of cracks
Blood oozing out of cracked feet
Became walking red flags
Became flowers showered by the city
Power cannot but bow down
To the unity of farmers, forests and flowing river.

13 March 2018
Translated by N. Venugopal

---

* Reference to Vijay Mallya and Nirav Modi, two corporate barons accused
  of availing loans worth thousands of crores from public-sector banks and
  fleeing the country.